Welcome to the world of Asterix!

The year is 50 BC. Gaul is entirely occupied by the Romans. Well, not entirely . . .
One small village of indomitable Gauls still holds out against the invaders.
And life is not easy for the Roman legionaries who garrison the fortified camps
of Totorum, Aquarium, Laudanum and Compendium . . .

Over to you!

Asterix is hidden in each of the scenes in this book. Are your powers of observation
really good? It's up to you to find our shrewd, cunning little hero – and there are
plenty of other surprises for you to spot as well!

The challenge:

Look carefully at the pages of this book – they are a real challenge!
Whenever you find Asterix, you win 2 laurel wreaths.
The other characters or things you are asked to track down score 1 laurel wreath each.
When you've finished, count up your winnings.
If you have won between 50 and 65 laurel wreaths, you're the champion!

And good luck, by Toutatis !

| Asterix | Obelix | Dogmatix | Getafix | Impedimenta | Unhygienix | Vitalstatistix | Cacofonix | Fulliautomatix |

| Mrs Fulliautomatix | Mrs Geriatrix | Geriatrix | Anticlimax | Cleopatra | Julius Caesar | Pirate lookout man | Pirate captain |

Where's Asterix?

IN THE GAULISH VILLAGE

The village is a hive of activity! All the Gauls are going about their business. How well do you know the villagers?

See if you can find:

Asterix
the most famous of all the Gauls

Obelix
his inseparable friend

Dogmatix
Obelix's faithful companion

Vitalstatistix
the chief of the tribe

Cacofonix
the village bard

Getafix
the venerable village druid

Score:
Laurel wreaths

x7

A FISH FIGHT

Starting the day with a good fish fight is a fine old Gaulish custom. As they say, there's no plaice like home. The Gauls keep fit with plenty of codswallop.

See if you can find:

Asterix

Geriatrix,
the oldest inhabitant of the village

Impedimenta,
wife of Chief Vitalstatistix

Obelix,
Asterix's best friend

Mrs Fulliautomatix,
the blacksmith's wife

A fish covered with red spots

Score:
Laurel wreaths

x7

A TRAFFIC JAM

The traffic is terrible in Lutetia, the capital of Gaul! Amphora-necks everywhere, and the streets are jammed with carts. The Gauls improvise a jam session to clear some Romans out of the way!

See if you can find:

Asterix

A Lutetian lady looking out of her window

Five flattened Romans suffering from concussion

Obelix rubbing his hands with glee

Score:
Laurel wreaths

x5

IN THE ARENA

Ladies and gentlemen, who's for some free punch? Anyone who lasts a round with Obelix will get plenty. Don't all push, there's enough for everyone . . .

See if you can find:

Asterix

Dogmatix

Two Gauls shaking hands

A little wooden horse on wheels

Score:
Laurel wreaths

x5

A BATTLE

Charge!
The Gauls are in charge,
the Romans are on the run!
Could a drop of
magic potion have anything
to do with this?

See if you can find:

Asterix

Julius Caesar,
Jules to his friends.

Mrs Fulliautomatix

Mrs Geriatrix

A Roman,
with a flower
between his teeth

Dogmatix,
putting the bite on a Roman

Score:
Laurel wreaths

x7

IN COURT

Obelix is up in court on criminal charges. This is a serious matter – the question that bothers him most is: when will they have a lunch break?

See if you can find:

Asterix

Four Roman legionaries playing musical instruments

A lady spectator with her hair in two plaits

Score:
Laurel wreaths

×4

ALL AT SEA

The poor pirates – some days their ship is sunk, other days it's boarded. They're right out of their depth. Only the Gauls are home and dry.

See if you can find:

Asterix

Four Romans jumping into the sea

A Roman putting his tongue out

The pirate captain

The pirate lookout man

Score:
Laurel wreaths

x6

FOR SALE ON
SPECIAL OFFER

It's slave-market day.
Ladies and gentlemen,
make your bids.
Everyone must go!

See if you can find:

Asterix

Cacofonix,
the village bard

The pirate lookout man

Score:
Laurel wreaths

×4

IN THE ROMAN LEGION

The Romans come bearing arms . . . but they've lost their bearings under all those shields! Better watch out for enemies!

See if you can find:

Asterix

Obelix in the middle of the battle

Two red shields

A chilly legionary wearing a scarf

Score:
Laurel wreaths

x5

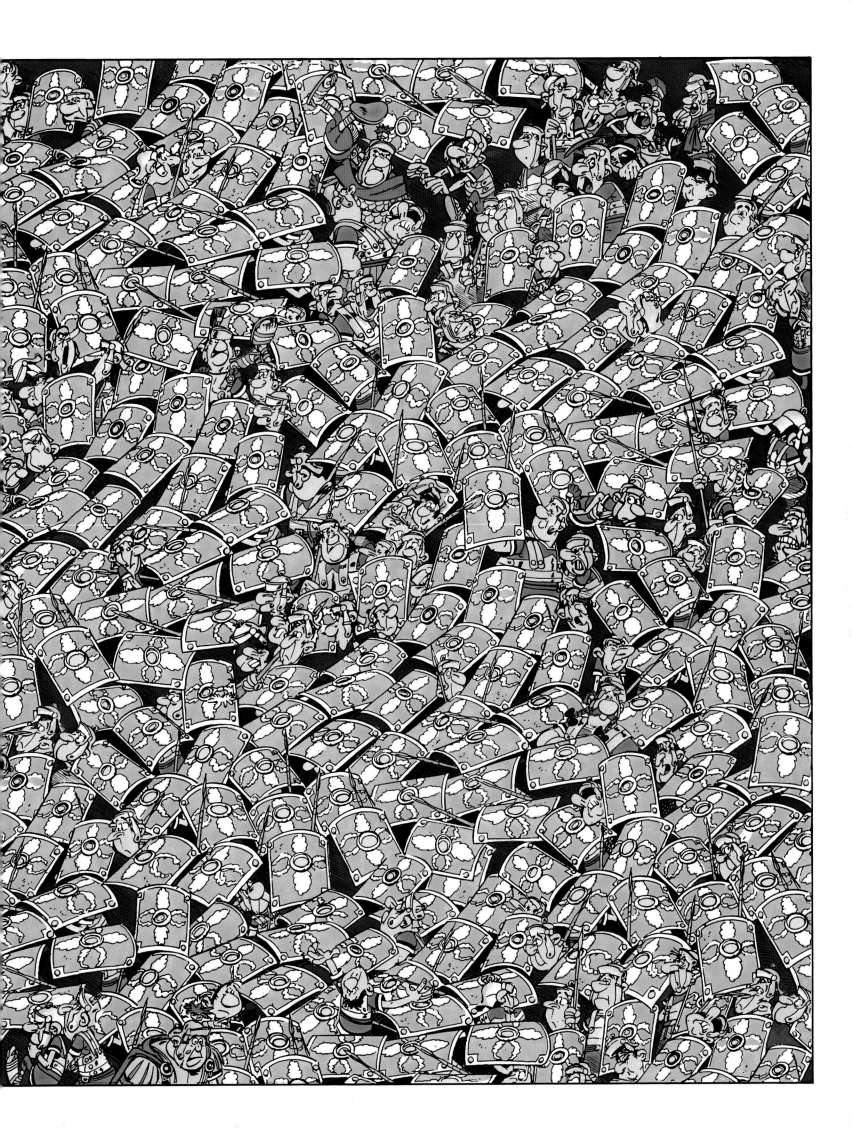

A PALACE FOR CAESAR

Cleopatra is supervising the building of a palace for Julius Caesar . . . and she dreams of throwing the architect Edifis to the crocodiles.

See if you can find:

Asterix

Cleopatra,
Queen of Egypt

A sarcophagus

Obelix and his obelisk

A leopard

Score:
Laurel wreaths :

x6

END OF PLAY?

The big match began so well, but it soon went downhill! When the Gauls joined in they kicked far too many goals.

See if you can find:

Asterix

The player in shirt no. 6

Anticlimax,
Asterix's first cousin once removed

Fulliautomatix,
the village blacksmith

Score:
Laurel wreaths

x5

THE TRADITIONAL BANQUET

Our heroes are glad to be back home in the little Gaulish village. All's well that ends well . . . except for Cacofonix, the victim of an incident beyond his control.

See if you can find:

Asterix

Two curious owls

Unhygienix,
the fishmonger

Score:
Laurel wreaths

x4

THE END

THE TRADITIONAL BANQUET

END OF PLAY?

A PALACE FOR CAESAR

IN THE ROMAN LEGION

FOR SALE ON SPECIAL OFFER

ALL AT SEA

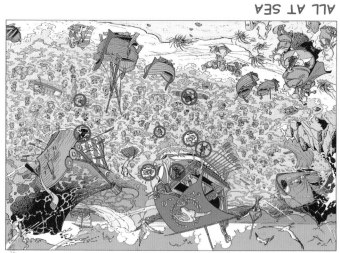

IN COURT

A BATTLE